IT'S TIME TO LEARN ABOUT ONLINE SIDE HUSTLES THAT MAKE THE MOST MONEY

It's Time to Learn about Online Side Hustles that Make the Most Money

Walter the Educator

Copyright © 2024 by Walter the Educator

All rights reserved. No part of this book may be reproduced in any manner whatsoever without written permission except in the case of brief quotations embodied in critical articles and reviews.

First Printing, 2024

Disclaimer

The author and publisher offer this information without warranties expressed or implied. No matter the grounds, neither the author nor the publisher will be accountable for any losses, injuries, or other damages caused by the reader's use of this book. Your use of this book acknowledges an understanding and acceptance of this disclaimer.

It's Time to Learn about Online Side Hustles that Make the Most Money is a collectible little learning book by Walter the Educator that belongs to the Little Learning Books Series. Collect them all and more books at WaltertheEducator.com

ONLINE SIDE HUSTLES THAT MAKE THE MOST MONEY

INTRO

In today's fast-paced and technology-driven world, the internet has opened countless doors for individuals looking to diversify their income streams. Online side hustles have become a popular option for those seeking to supplement their income or even replace their traditional 9-to-5 jobs. Whether you're a full-time employee looking for extra cash, a stay-at-home parent needing a flexible job, or an entrepreneur seeking to fund a larger venture, online side hustles provide flexible, scalable, and often low-barrier opportunities to make money. This little book explores the most profitable online side hustles, how they work, and what makes them successful.

1. Freelance Writing

Freelance writing is one of the most popular online side hustles, offering substantial income potential for those with a talent for words. Content is the backbone of the internet, and businesses are constantly in need of blog posts, web copy, email marketing campaigns, product descriptions, and more.

It's Time to Learn about
Online Side Hustles that Make the Most Money

Platforms like Upwork, Fiverr, and Freelancer have made it easy for writers to connect with clients worldwide. Freelance writers can earn anywhere from $20 to $100 or more per article, depending on their skill level, niche, and experience. Specialized writers, such as those in technology, healthcare, or finance, often command higher rates.

It's Time to Learn about

Online Side Hustles that Make the Most Money

To succeed, writers must hone their craft, maintain a portfolio of their work, and consistently market themselves. Developing a niche is key to earning top dollar, as clients are willing to pay more for experts in specific areas. For example, technical writing, medical writing, and SEO copywriting often yield higher-paying gigs.

It's Time to Learn about

Online Side Hustles that Make the Most Money

2. Online Tutoring and Teaching

The demand for online education has exploded in recent years, and platforms like VIPKid, Teachable, and Udemy have given educators and subject matter experts a place to share their knowledge. Online tutoring is especially lucrative in subjects like math, science, and English as a second language (ESL), where there's an ongoing demand for qualified instructors.

It's Time to Learn about

Online Side Hustles that Make the Most Money

Online tutors can set their own hours and rates, with many earning between $20 and $60 per hour, depending on their qualifications and the subjects they teach. Some instructors opt to create and sell courses on platforms like Teachable or Udemy, which allows them to generate passive income. By investing time in creating high-quality course materials, educators can sell these courses indefinitely, earning a steady income without needing to teach live classes continuously.

It's Time to Learn about

Online Side Hustles that Make the Most Money

3. Dropshipping

Dropshipping is an eCommerce model where entrepreneurs sell products to customers without holding any inventory. When a customer places an order, the seller buys the product from a third party, usually a wholesaler or manufacturer, who ships the item directly to the customer.

It's Time to Learn about
Online Side Hustles that Make the Most Money

This business model has gained traction because of its low startup costs and scalability. Aspiring entrepreneurs can set up a dropshipping store using platforms like Shopify or WooCommerce with minimal investment. Successful dropshippers often focus on finding a niche product or market, using social media marketing and SEO techniques to drive traffic to their stores.

It's Time to Learn about

Online Side Hustles that Make the Most Money

While dropshipping offers the potential for significant income, it also comes with challenges. Margins can be thin, especially in highly competitive markets, and customer service can be tricky when sellers rely on third parties to fulfill orders. Despite these hurdles, some dropshippers earn six-figure incomes by scaling their businesses and using strategic marketing techniques.

It's Time to Learn about

Online Side Hustles that Make the Most Money

4. Print-on-Demand (POD)

Similar to dropshipping, print-on-demand (POD) is a low-risk eCommerce business model where entrepreneurs sell custom-designed products, such as T-shirts, mugs, phone cases, and more. With POD, sellers create designs and upload them to platforms like Printful, Redbubble, or Teespring, which handle printing, shipping, and customer service.

It's Time to Learn about Online Side Hustles that Make the Most Money

This business model is attractive because it requires no upfront inventory, and sellers only pay for the production of items that have been sold. POD businesses thrive on creativity and marketing.

It's Time to Learn about Online Side Hustles that Make the Most Money

Successful sellers often focus on creating niche designs that appeal to specific audiences, such as sports enthusiasts, pet lovers, or fans of pop culture.

It's Time to Learn about

Online Side Hustles that Make the Most Money

With effective social media marketing, especially on Instagram and Pinterest, POD entrepreneurs can create a loyal following and generate significant revenue. Though individual profit margins may be lower compared to other business models, the ability to scale quickly makes this a lucrative side hustle.

It's Time to Learn about

Online Side Hustles that Make the Most Money

5. Affiliate Marketing

Affiliate marketing allows individuals to earn commissions by promoting other people's products or services. This model is appealing because it requires little to no upfront investment. Affiliate marketers promote products through websites, blogs, or social media, earning a percentage of sales when someone makes a purchase through their referral link.

It's Time to Learn about

Online Side Hustles that Make the Most Money

To become a successful affiliate marketer, individuals must choose products or services that align with their audience or niche. Popular affiliate networks include Amazon Associates, ShareASale, and CJ Affiliate, where marketers can find products to promote in various categories.

It's Time to Learn about

Online Side Hustles that Make the Most Money

Building a strong personal brand or a blog with valuable content can help affiliate marketers grow their income.

It's Time to Learn about
Online Side Hustles that Make the Most Money

Top-performing affiliates use SEO, email marketing, and paid advertising to increase traffic to their referral links, driving more sales and earning higher commissions. High-tier affiliates can earn six or even seven figures annually by leveraging their audience and promoting high-ticket items.

It's Time to Learn about

Online Side Hustles that Make the Most Money

6. Social Media Management

As businesses recognize the importance of maintaining an online presence, the demand for social media managers has skyrocketed. Many small businesses and entrepreneurs don't have the time or expertise to manage their social media accounts, which has created opportunities for freelancers and part-time social media managers.

It's Time to Learn about Online Side Hustles that Make the Most Money

Social media managers handle tasks like content creation, scheduling posts, responding to comments, running ads, and analyzing performance metrics on platforms like Instagram, Facebook, Twitter, and LinkedIn. Depending on experience, social media managers can earn between $15 to $100 per hour. Those who specialize in social media advertising, particularly Facebook and Instagram ads, often command higher rates.

It's Time to Learn about Online Side Hustles that Make the Most Money

Building a successful social media management business requires creativity, strategic thinking, and a deep understanding of each platform's algorithms and best practices. By helping businesses grow their online presence, social media managers can build a profitable side hustle or even transition to a full-time career.

It's Time to Learn about

Online Side Hustles that Make the Most Money

7. YouTube and Content Creation

Content creation, particularly on YouTube, has become one of the most lucrative online side hustles. YouTubers make money through ads, sponsorships, and selling their own products or services. Successful creators can earn thousands of dollars per month, with top-tier influencers making millions annually.

It's Time to Learn about

Online Side Hustles that Make the Most Money

To start a YouTube channel, creators must focus on producing engaging and valuable content that resonates with their audience.

It's Time to Learn about

Online Side Hustles that Make the Most Money

Niche channels, such as those focused on tech reviews, personal finance, fitness, or lifestyle, often do well because they cater to specific interests. Consistency and authenticity are critical in building an audience, and as subscribers and views grow, so does the potential for monetization.

It's Time to Learn about Online Side Hustles that Make the Most Money

Besides YouTube, content creators can also explore platforms like TikTok, Instagram, and podcasts to build their brand and audience. Diversifying content streams and maintaining multiple channels can lead to even greater income opportunities.

It's Time to Learn about

Online Side Hustles that Make the Most Money

8. Selling Digital Products

Selling digital products like eBooks, templates, graphics, and online courses has become increasingly popular. Digital products have the advantage of being scalable, meaning once a product is created, it can be sold indefinitely without needing to invest additional time or resources.

It's Time to Learn about

Online Side Hustles that Make the Most Money

Digital products cater to a wide variety of niches, including photography, web design, marketing, and more.

It's Time to Learn about
Online Side Hustles that Make the Most Money

Platforms like Etsy, Gumroad, and Creative Market allow creators to sell their products easily. For example, graphic designers can sell website templates or social media graphics, while writers can publish and sell eBooks.

It's Time to Learn about

Online Side Hustles that Make the Most Money

The key to success in selling digital products is creating high-quality, in-demand content and effectively marketing it to the right audience. Many entrepreneurs also create bundled products, increasing the perceived value and offering customers a better deal, which can lead to more sales.

It's Time to Learn about

Online Side Hustles that Make the Most Money

9. Virtual Assistance

As more businesses operate online, the need for virtual assistants (VAs) has grown substantially. Virtual assistants provide administrative, technical, or creative support to businesses and entrepreneurs remotely. Common tasks include managing emails, scheduling appointments, handling customer service, managing social media, and conducting research.

It's Time to Learn about

Online Side Hustles that Make the Most Money

VAs can work part-time or full-time and typically charge hourly rates ranging from $10 to $50, depending on their skills and experience. Specialized VAs who offer services like project management, bookkeeping, or marketing support often command higher rates.

It's Time to Learn about Online Side Hustles that Make the Most Money

Freelancing platforms like Upwork and Freelancer make it easy for virtual assistants to find clients, but building long-term relationships and networking within the business community can lead to more stable and higher-paying gigs.

It's Time to Learn about

Online Side Hustles that Make the Most Money

10. Stock Photography and Videography

Stock photography and videography are excellent side hustles for creative individuals who have a passion for visual arts. Websites like Shutterstock, Adobe Stock, and iStock allow photographers and videographers to sell their work to individuals, businesses, and media outlets around the world.

It's Time to Learn about Online Side Hustles that Make the Most Money

While this side hustle may take time to build a portfolio and gain traction, it can become a source of passive income. Each time someone licenses one of your photos or videos, you earn a royalty.

It's Time to Learn about

Online Side Hustles that Make the Most Money

By creating high-quality, in-demand content, such as lifestyle images, business settings, or travel footage, photographers and videographers can make a significant income over time.

It's Time to Learn about

Online Side Hustles that Make the Most Money

11. Online Coaching and Consulting

Online coaching and consulting have become profitable ventures for experts in various fields, from business and finance to health and wellness. Coaches offer personalized guidance and support to clients seeking to achieve specific goals, while consultants provide expert advice to businesses looking to improve performance.

It's Time to Learn about Online Side Hustles that Make the Most Money

Coaches and consultants can charge premium rates for one-on-one sessions, group coaching, or even digital courses. Platforms like Zoom, Skype, or Teachable make it easy to connect with clients globally. Successful coaches and consultants often have years of experience or certification in their area of expertise, allowing them to command higher fees.

It's Time to Learn about

Online Side Hustles that Make the Most Money

Building a strong personal brand, growing an audience, and offering valuable insights are essential for growing an online coaching or consulting business. As a side hustle, it offers flexibility, scalability, and substantial income potential.

It's Time to Learn about

Online Side Hustles that Make the Most Money

12. App Development and Software Creation

With the rise of mobile technology and digital services, app development and software creation have become highly profitable online side hustles for individuals with technical expertise. Freelance developers can create mobile apps, websites, or custom software solutions for clients or develop their own apps and monetize them through app stores or advertising.

It's Time to Learn about

Online Side Hustles that Make the Most Money

Even without extensive coding knowledge, platforms like Bubble and Glide allow entrepreneurs to build no-code apps. Developers who possess coding skills, however, have the advantage of creating more sophisticated and unique solutions, which can command higher fees.

It's Time to Learn about Online Side Hustles that Make the Most Money

The tech industry is continually growing, and businesses of all sizes are looking for custom solutions to improve efficiency and customer experience. Successful developers focus on solving specific problems within their niche, creating apps that fill gaps in the market.

It's Time to Learn about

Online Side Hustles that Make the Most Money

OUTRO

Online side hustles offer a wide array of opportunities for individuals to earn extra income, build skills, and even develop full-time careers. Whether you're interested in freelancing, eCommerce, content creation, or providing specialized services, the internet offers endless possibilities. Success in online side hustles requires dedication, a willingness to learn, and strategic thinking. By identifying your strengths and finding a profitable niche, you can turn your side hustle into a steady income stream or even a thriving business.

ABOUT THE CREATOR

Walter the Educator is one of the pseudonyms for Walter Anderson. Formally educated in Chemistry, Business, and Education, he is an educator, an author, a diverse entrepreneur, and he is the son of a disabled war veteran. "Walter the Educator" shares his time between educating and creating. He holds interests and owns several creative projects that entertain, enlighten, enhance, and educate, hoping to inspire and motivate you. Follow, find new works, and stay up to date with Walter the Educator™

at WaltertheEducator.com

Milton Keynes UK
Ingram Content Group UK Ltd.
UKHW030909141024
449705UK00013B/641